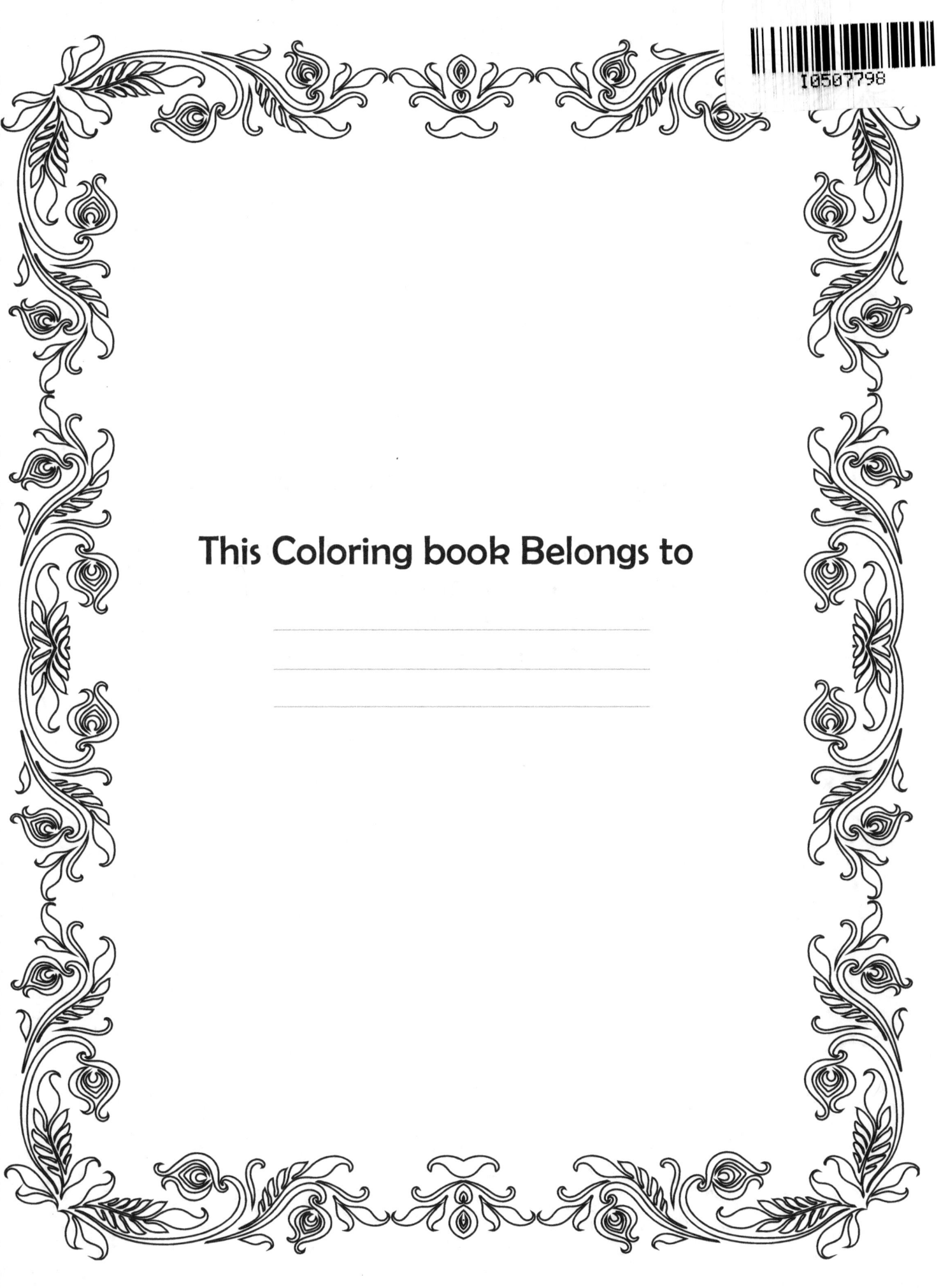

This Coloring book Belongs to

Copyright 2020 – All rights reserved

This book or any portion thereof may not be reproduced or used in any manner whatsoever without the express written permission of the publisher except for the use of brief quotations in a book review.

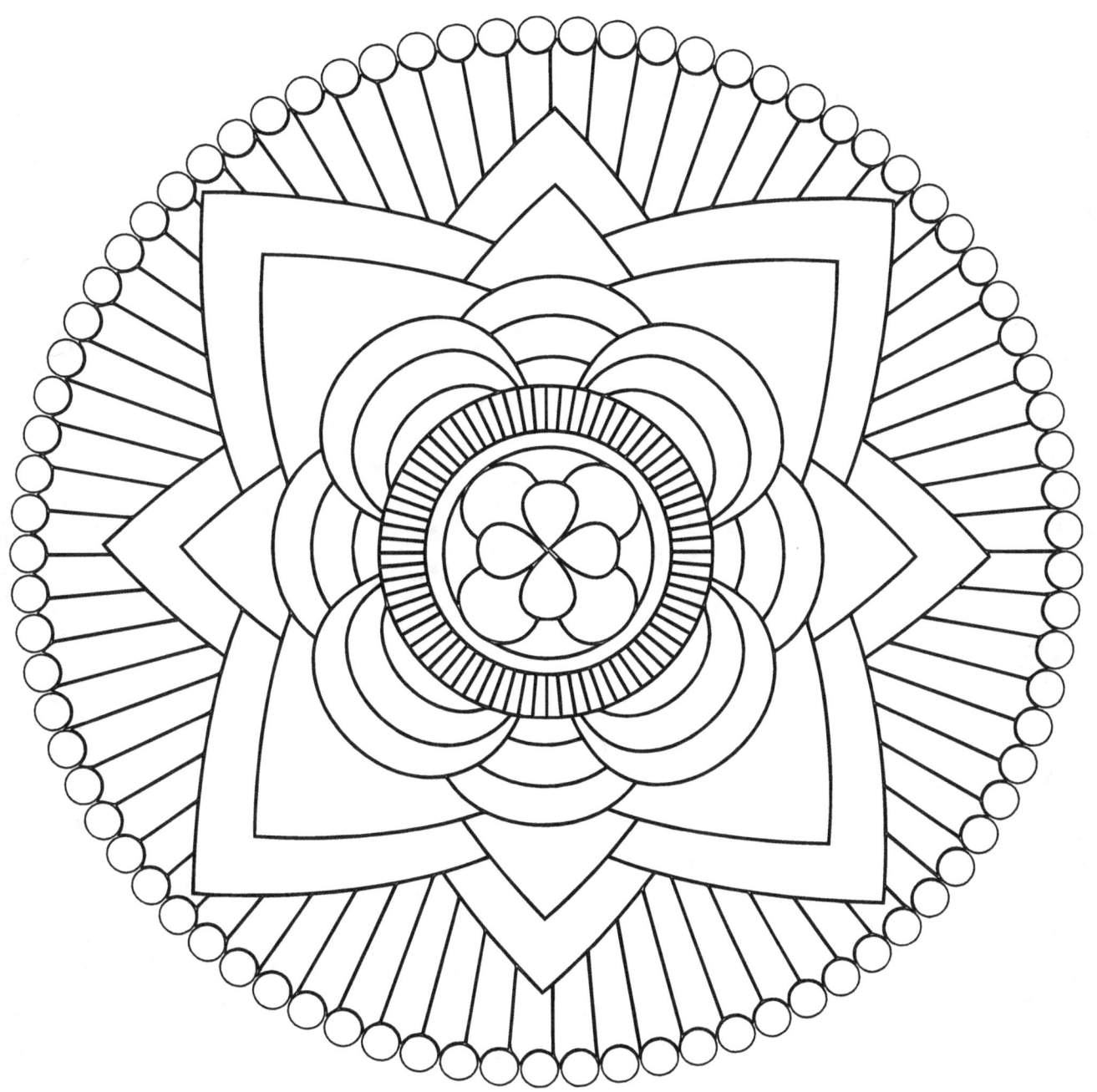

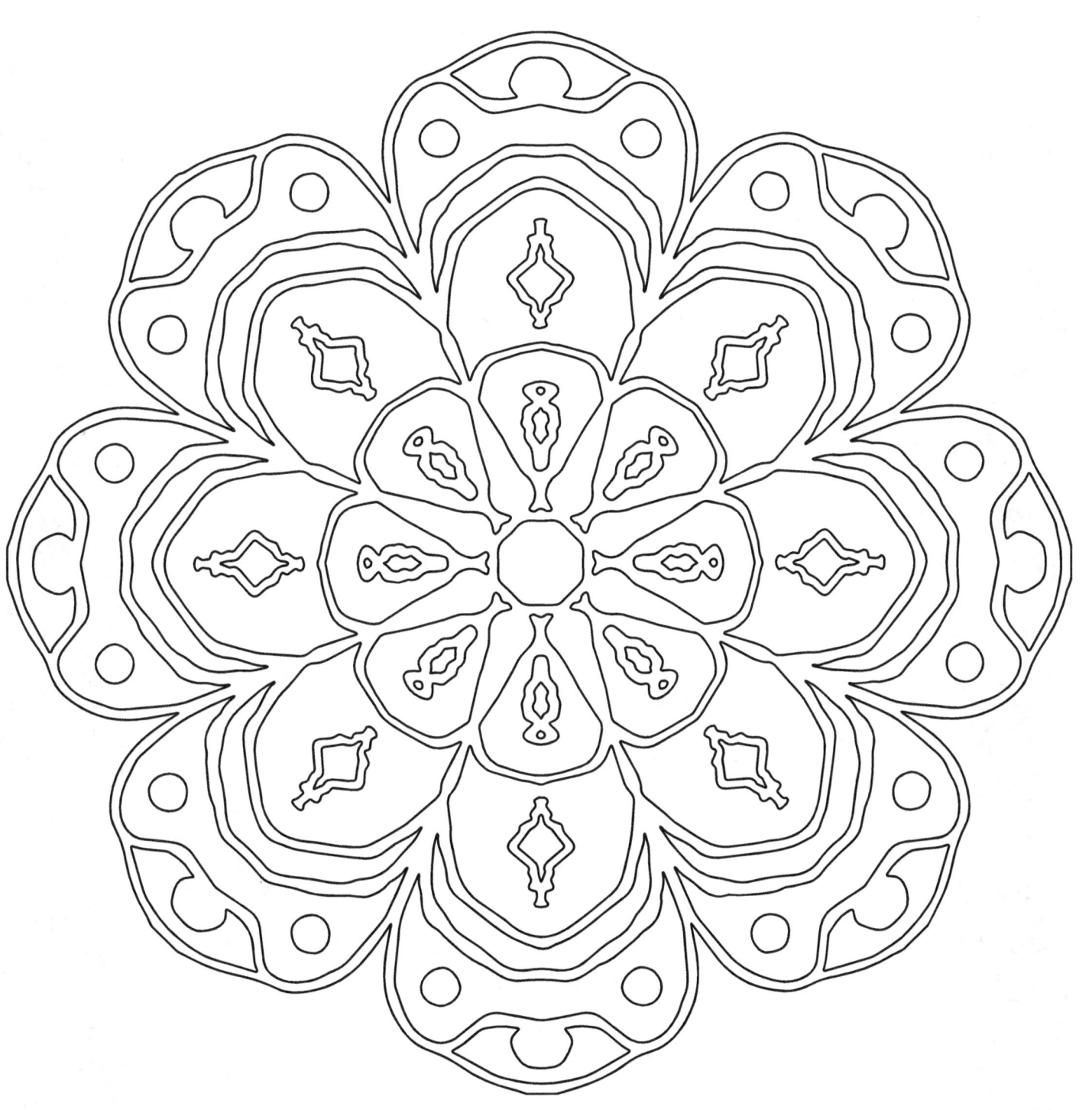

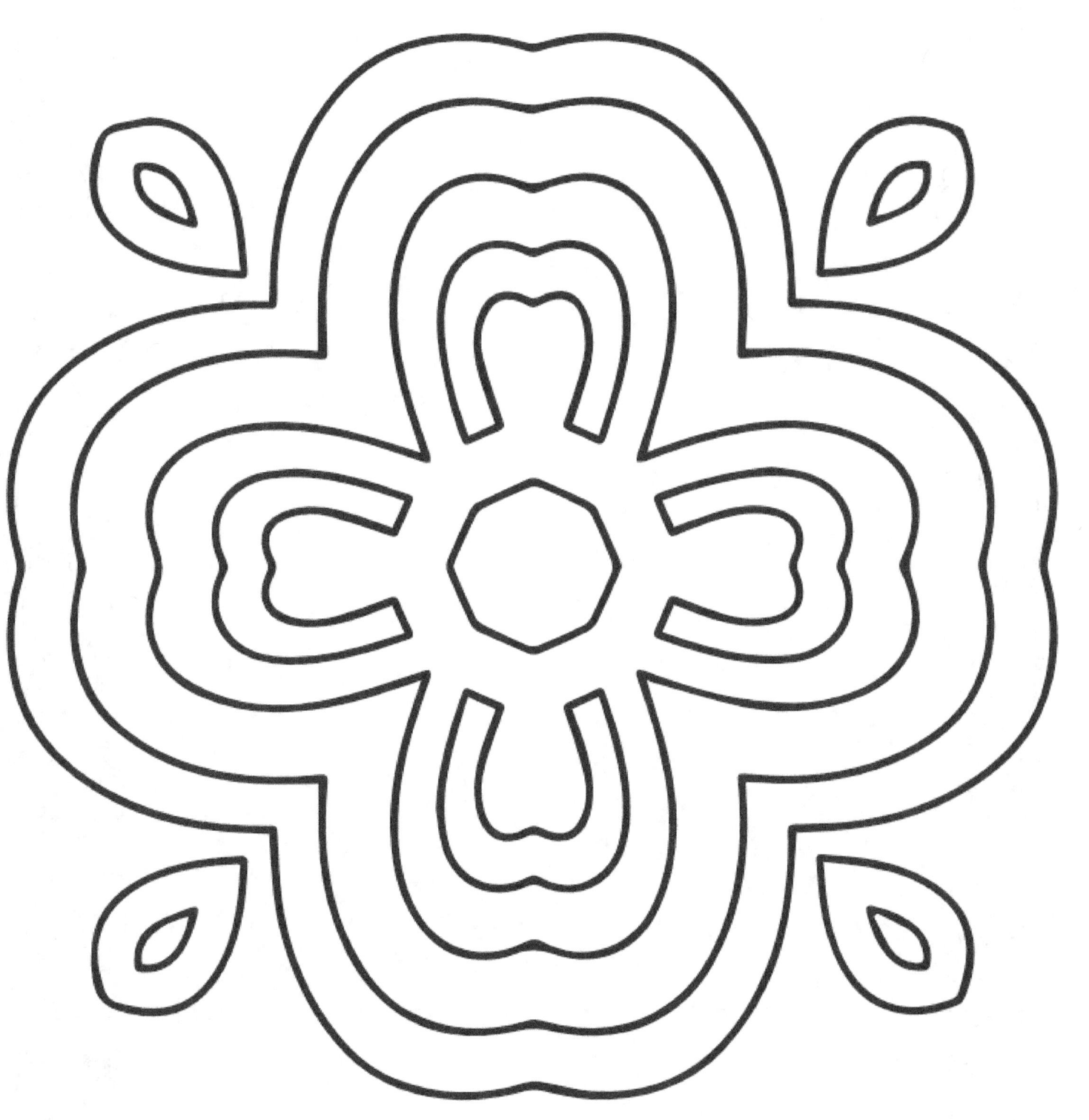

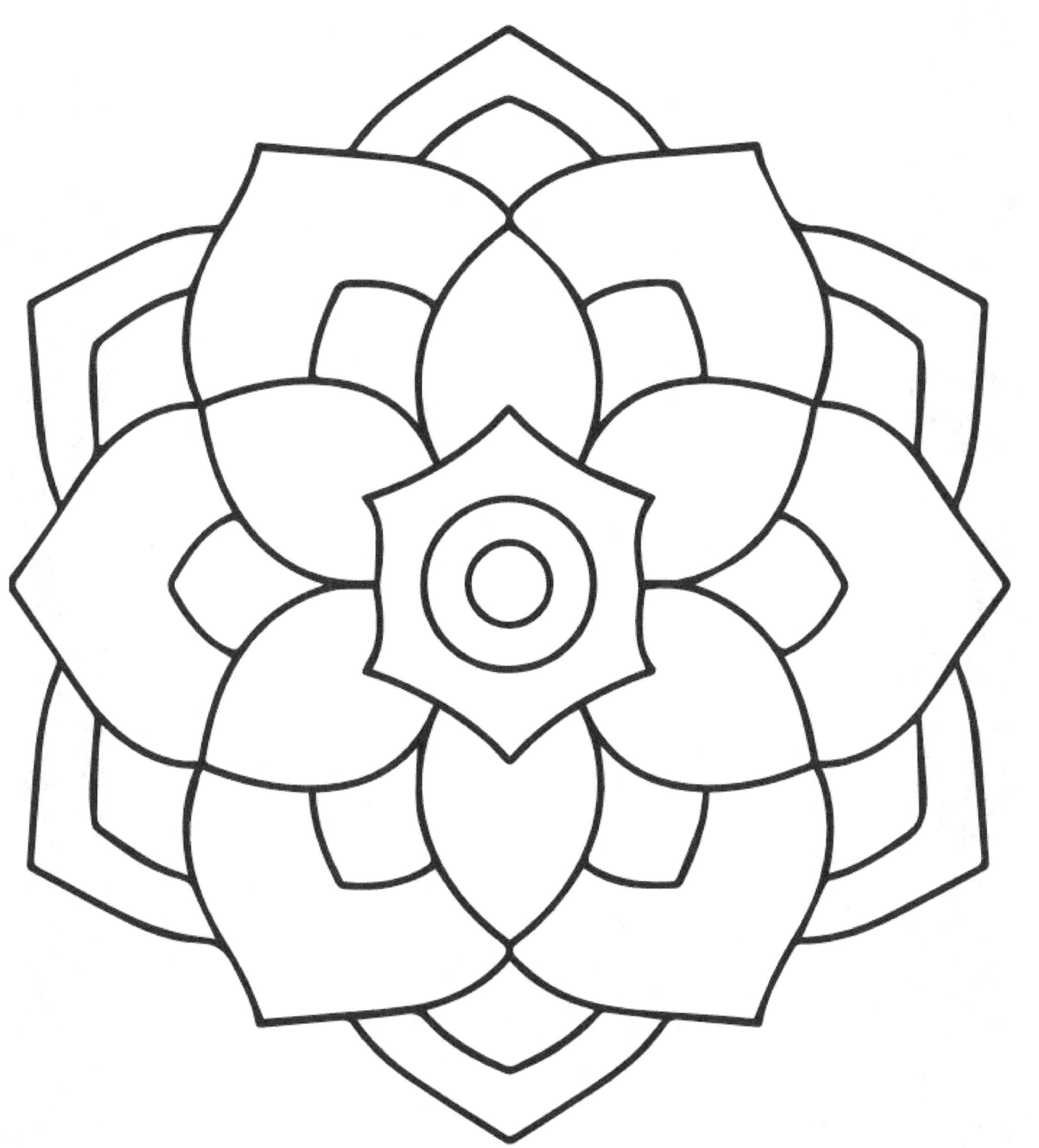

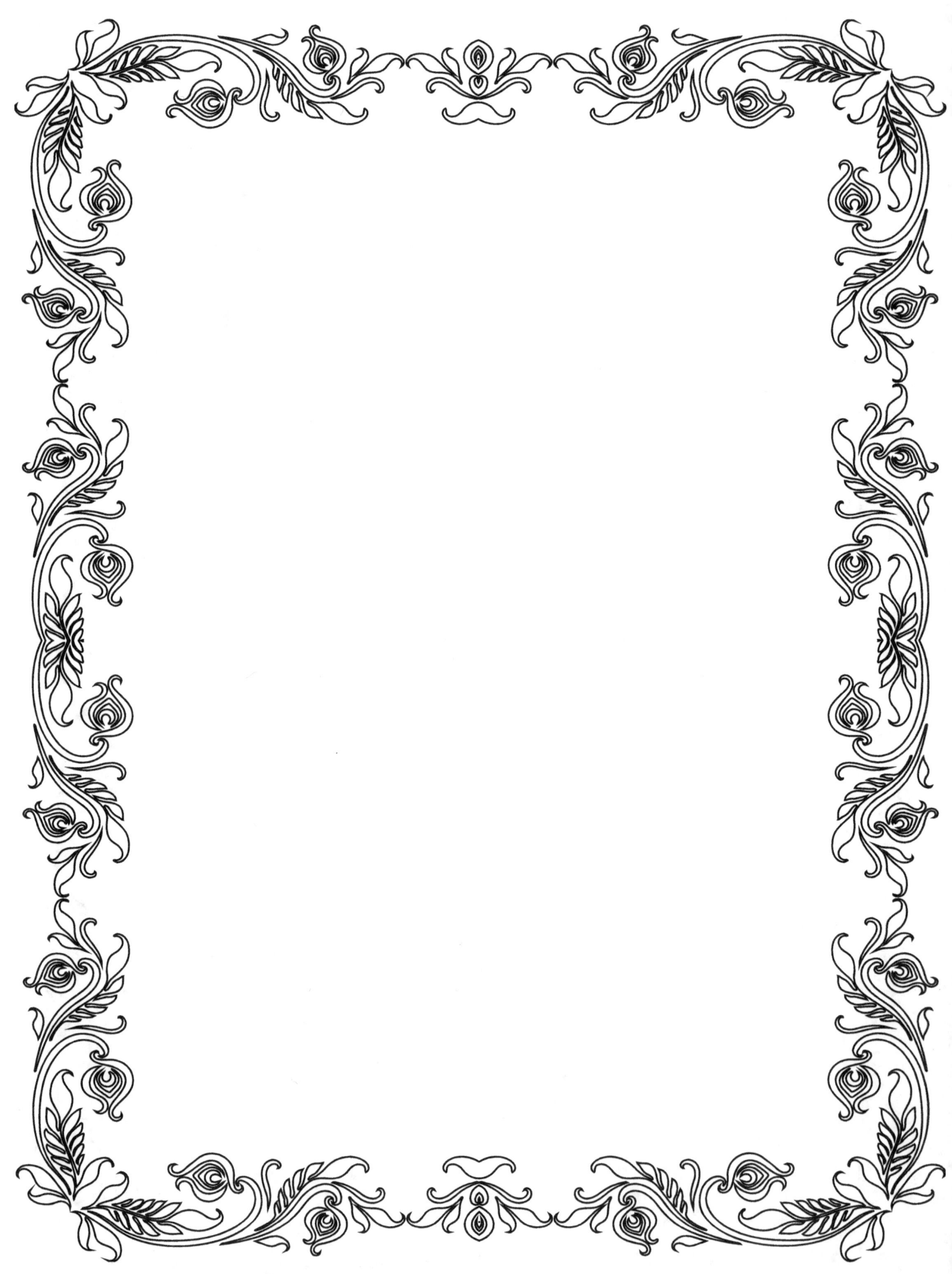

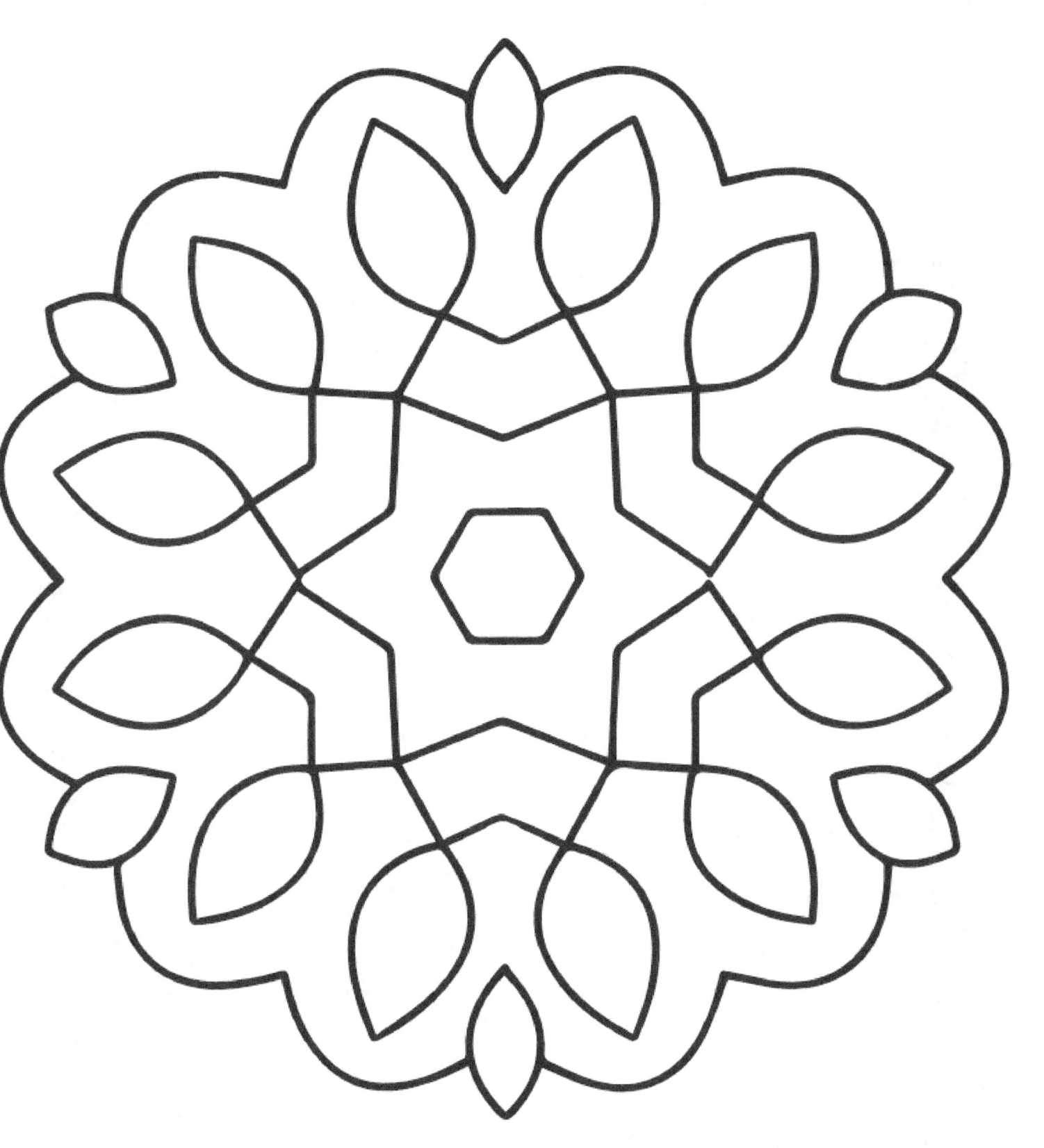

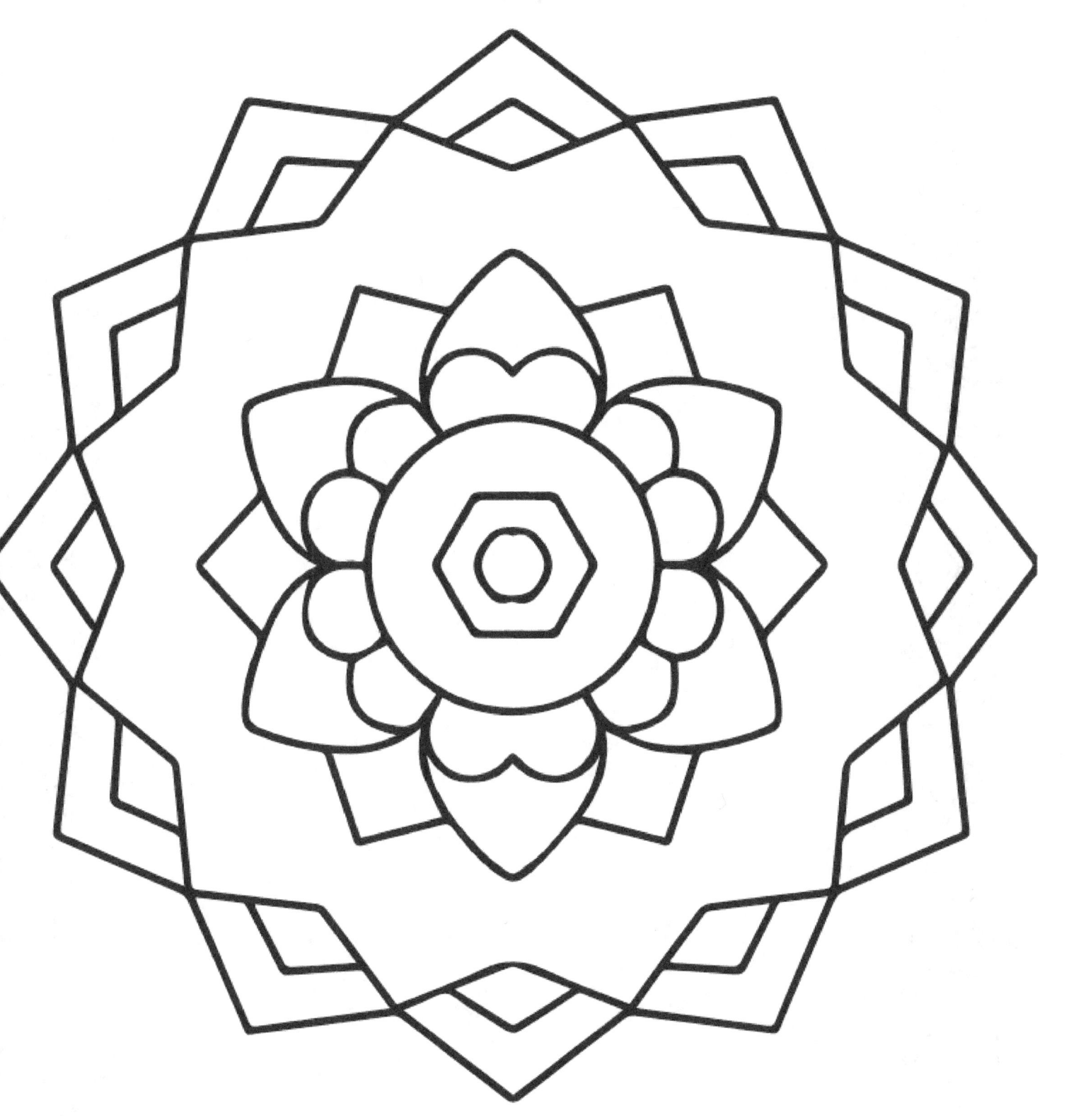

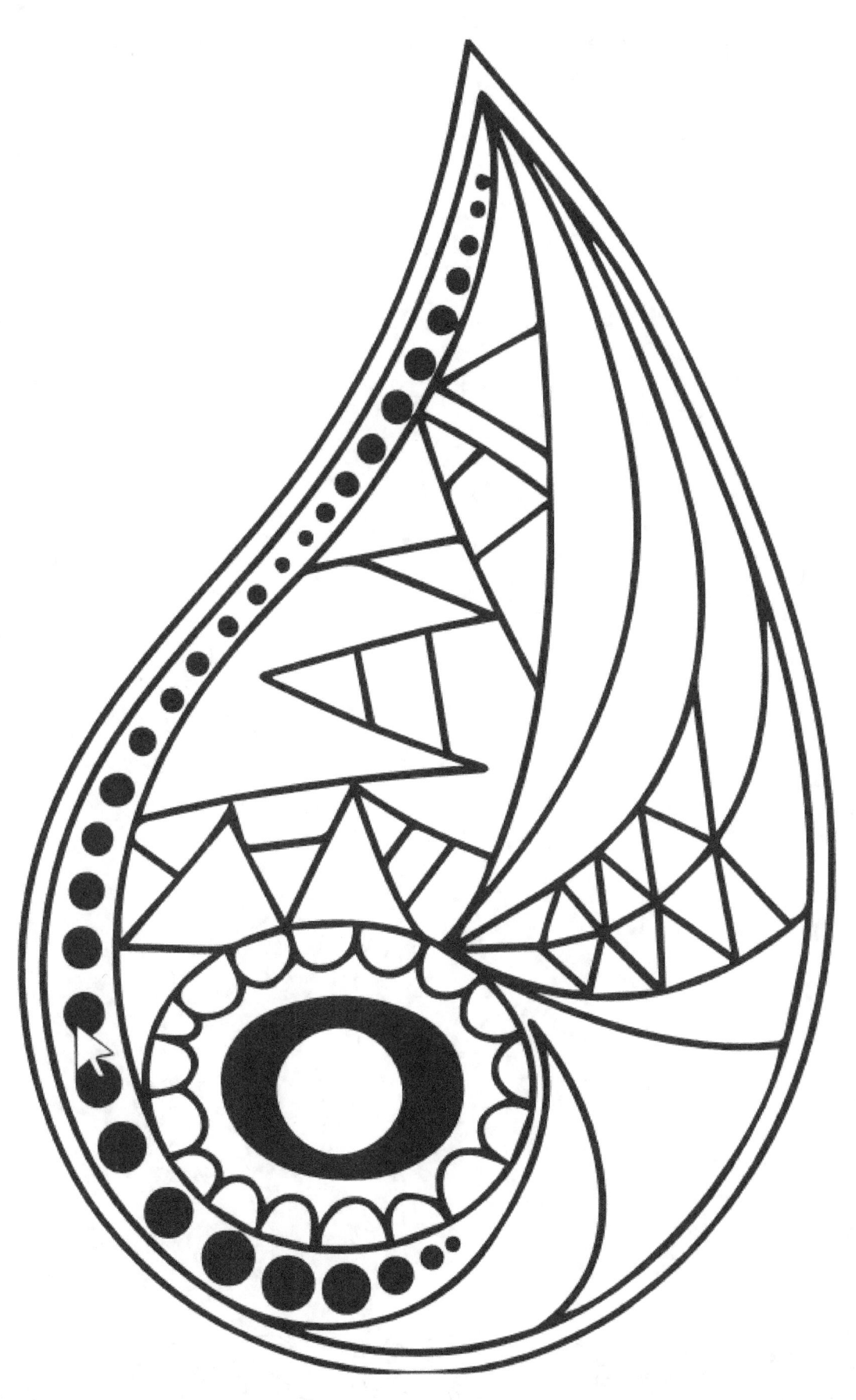

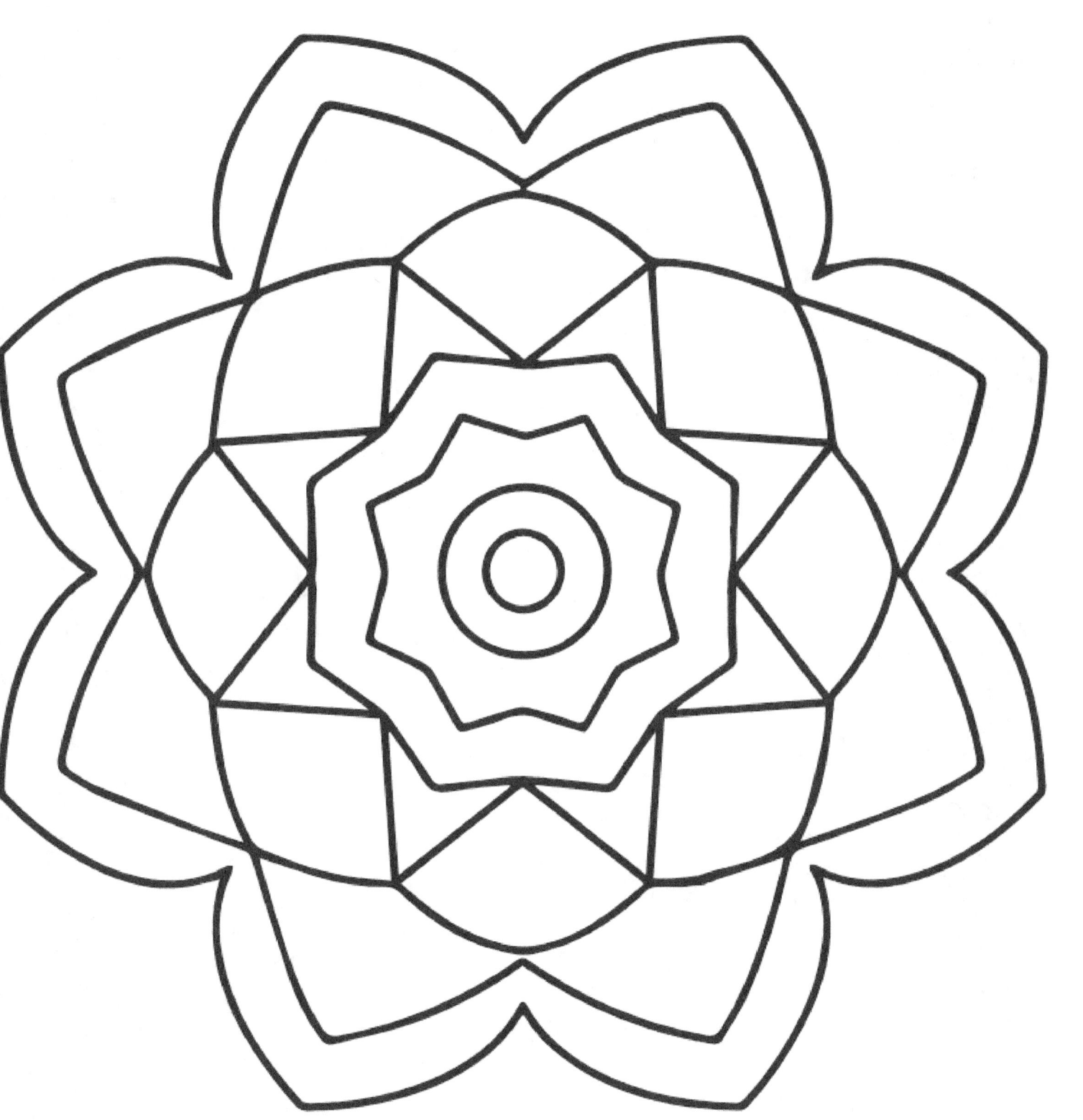

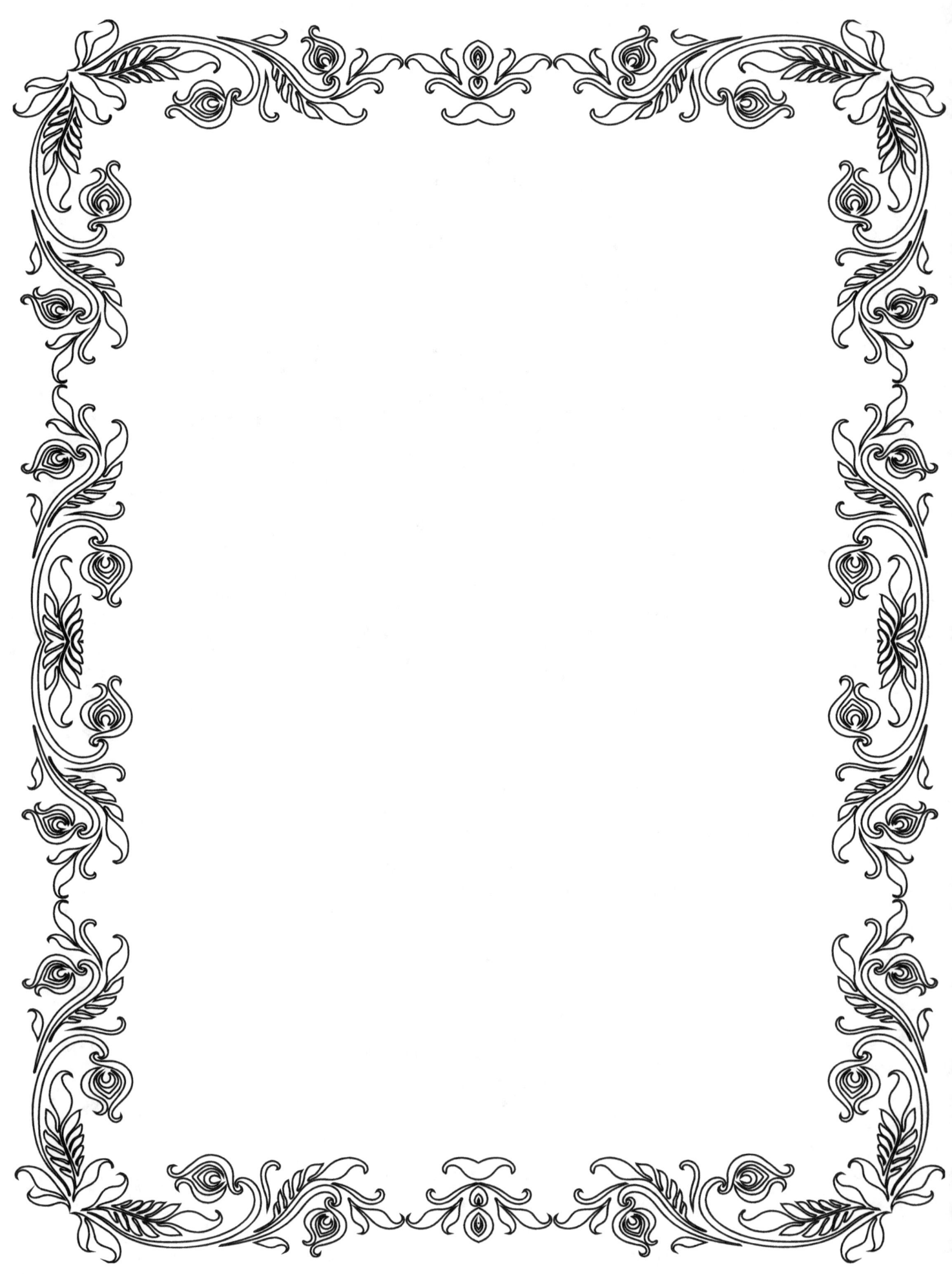

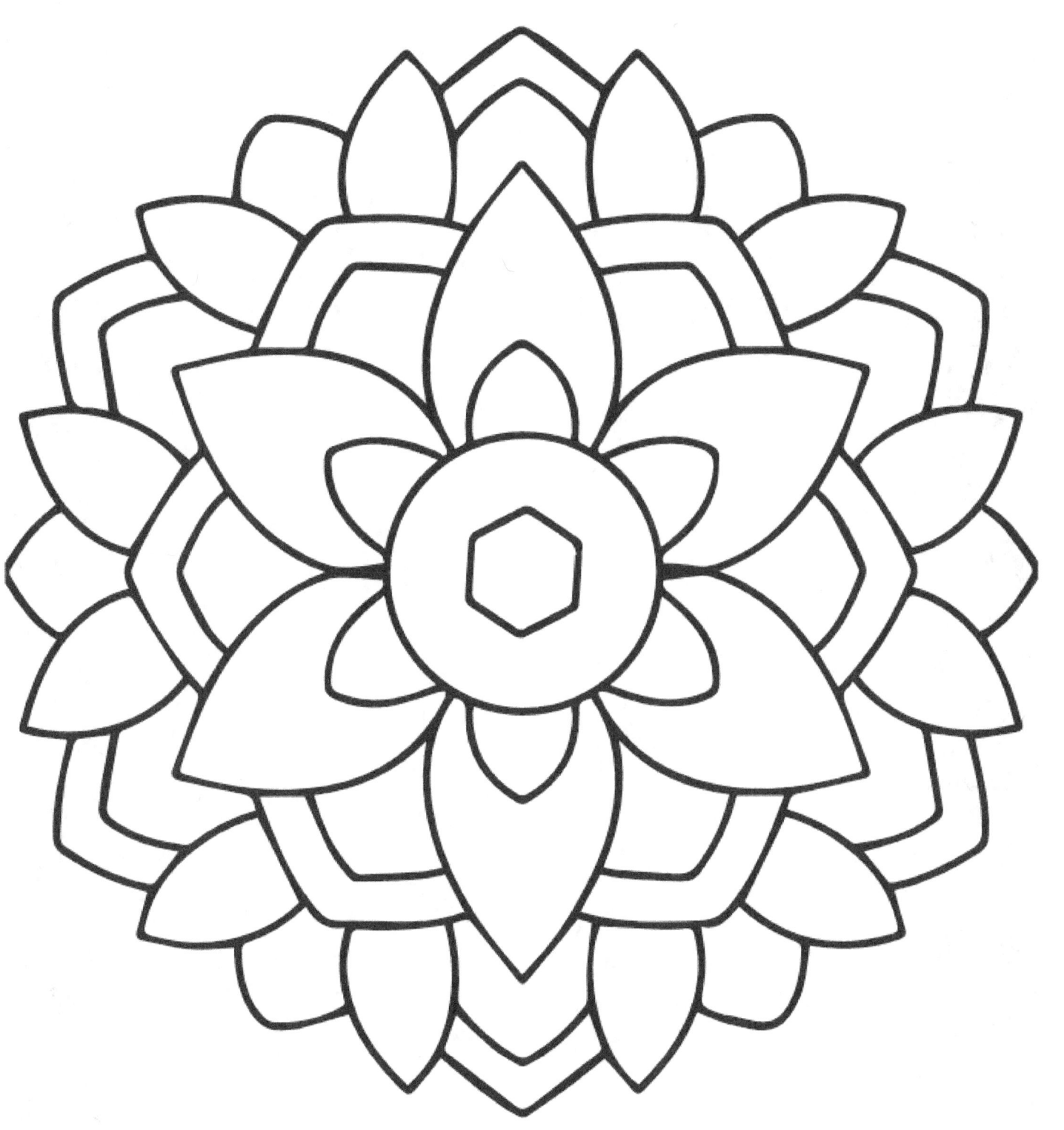

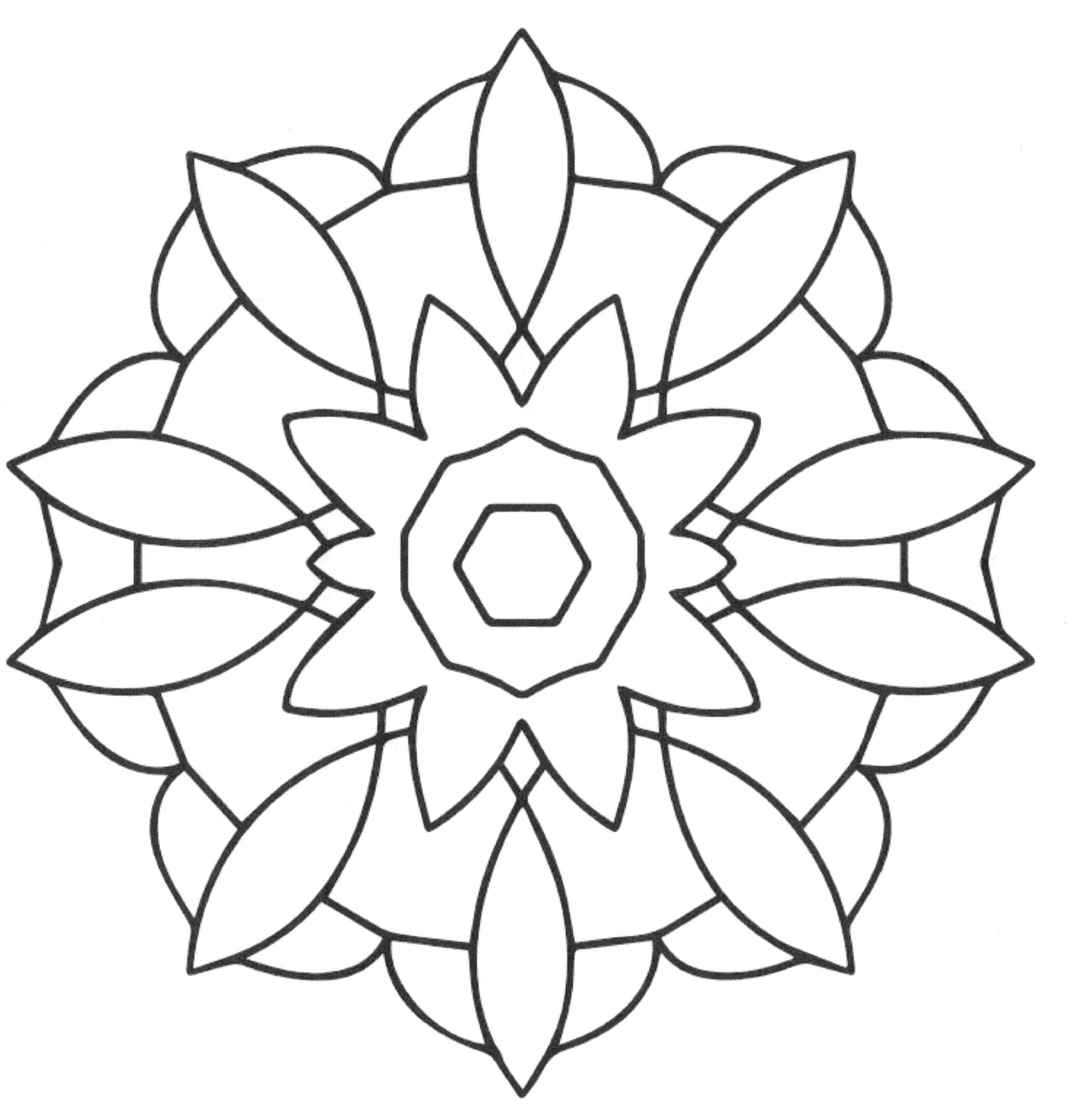

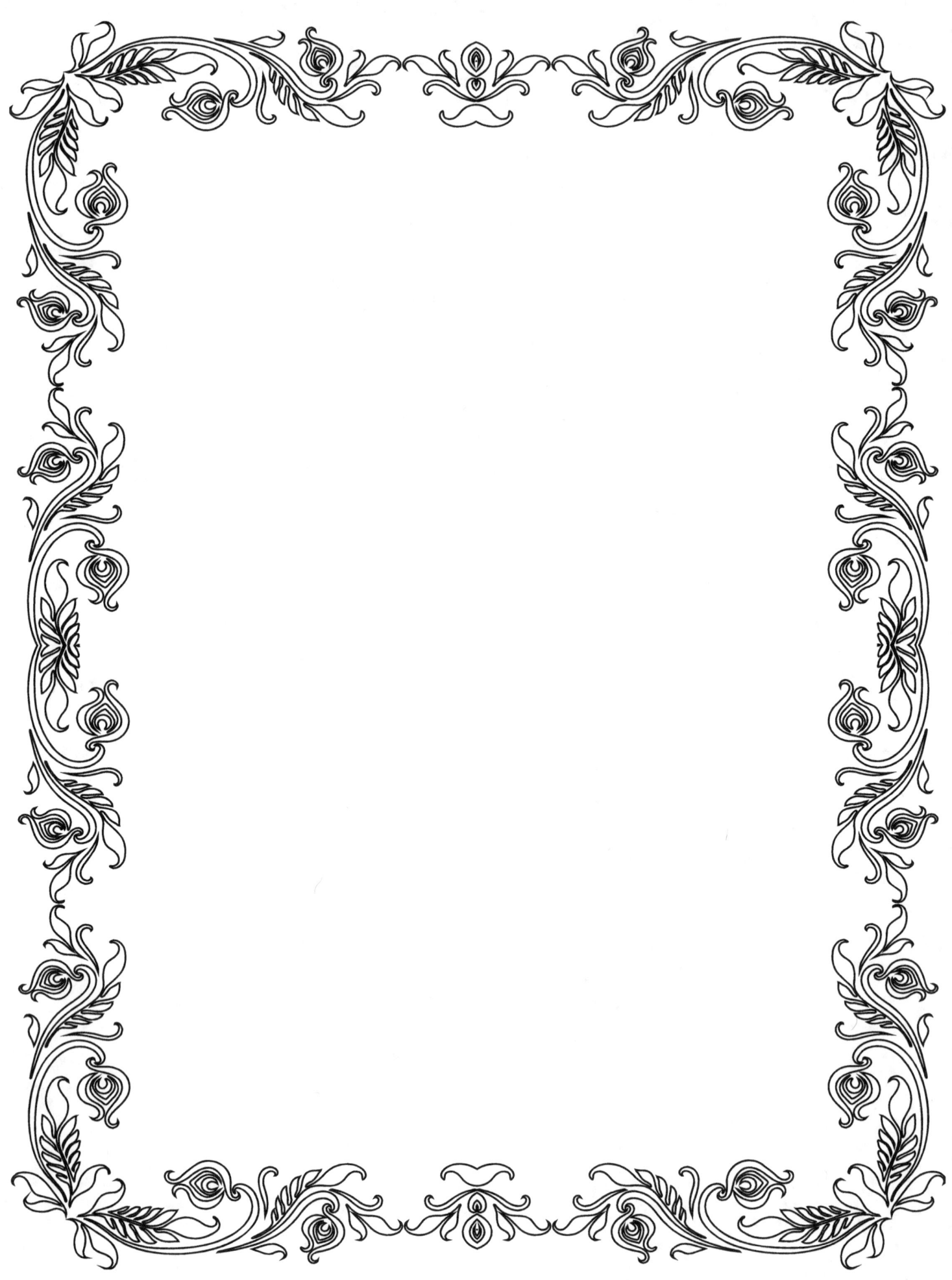

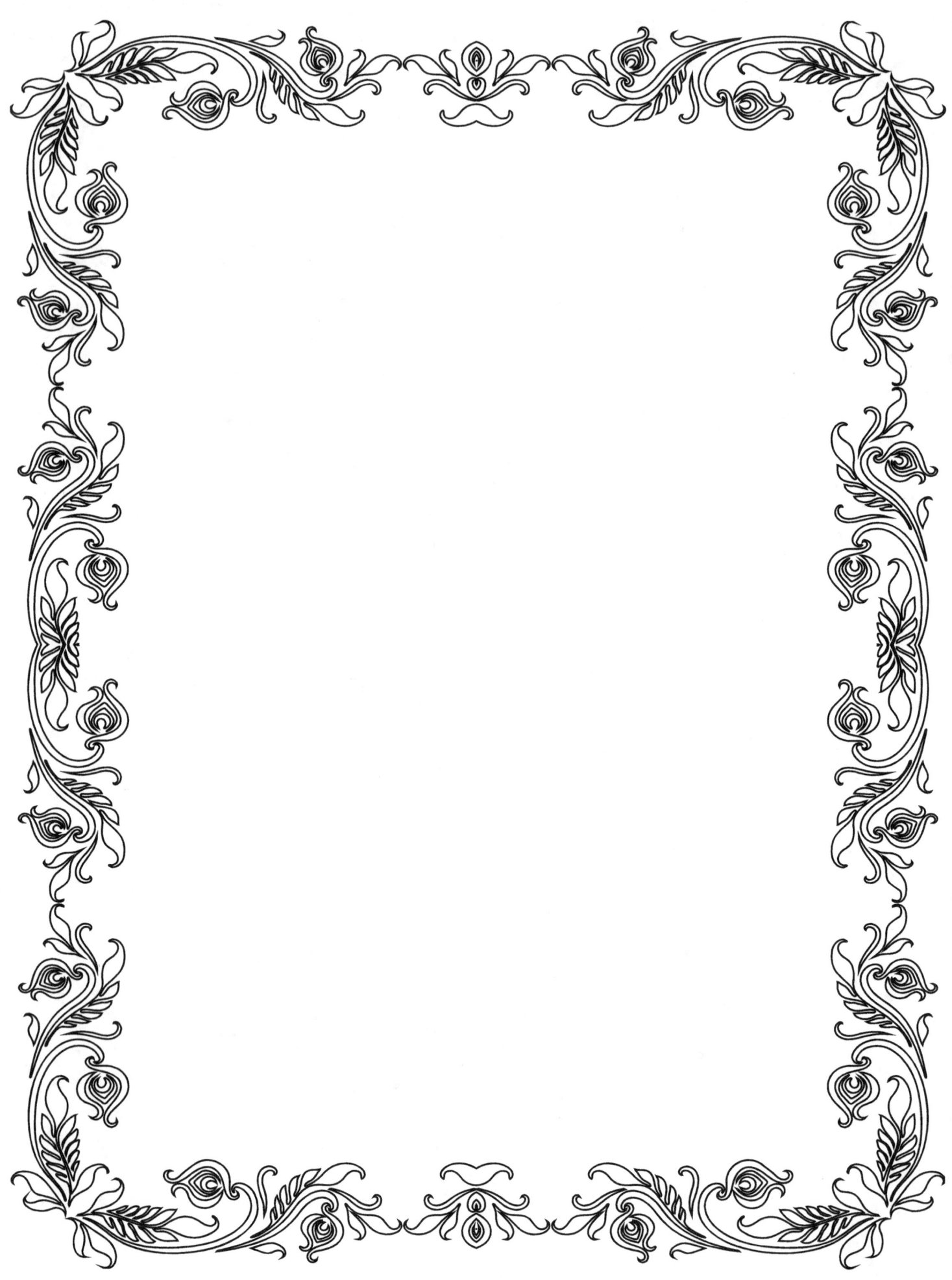

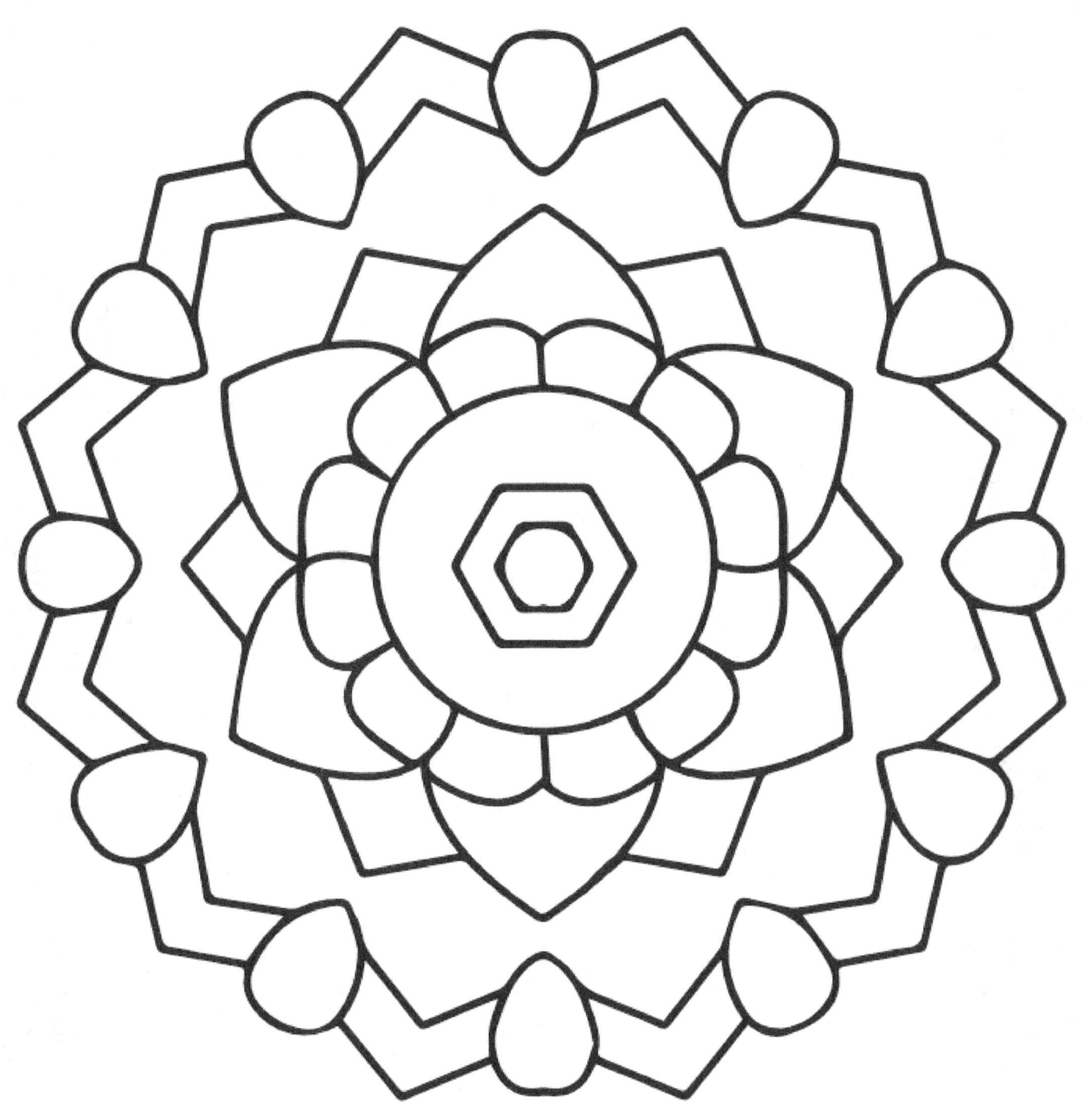

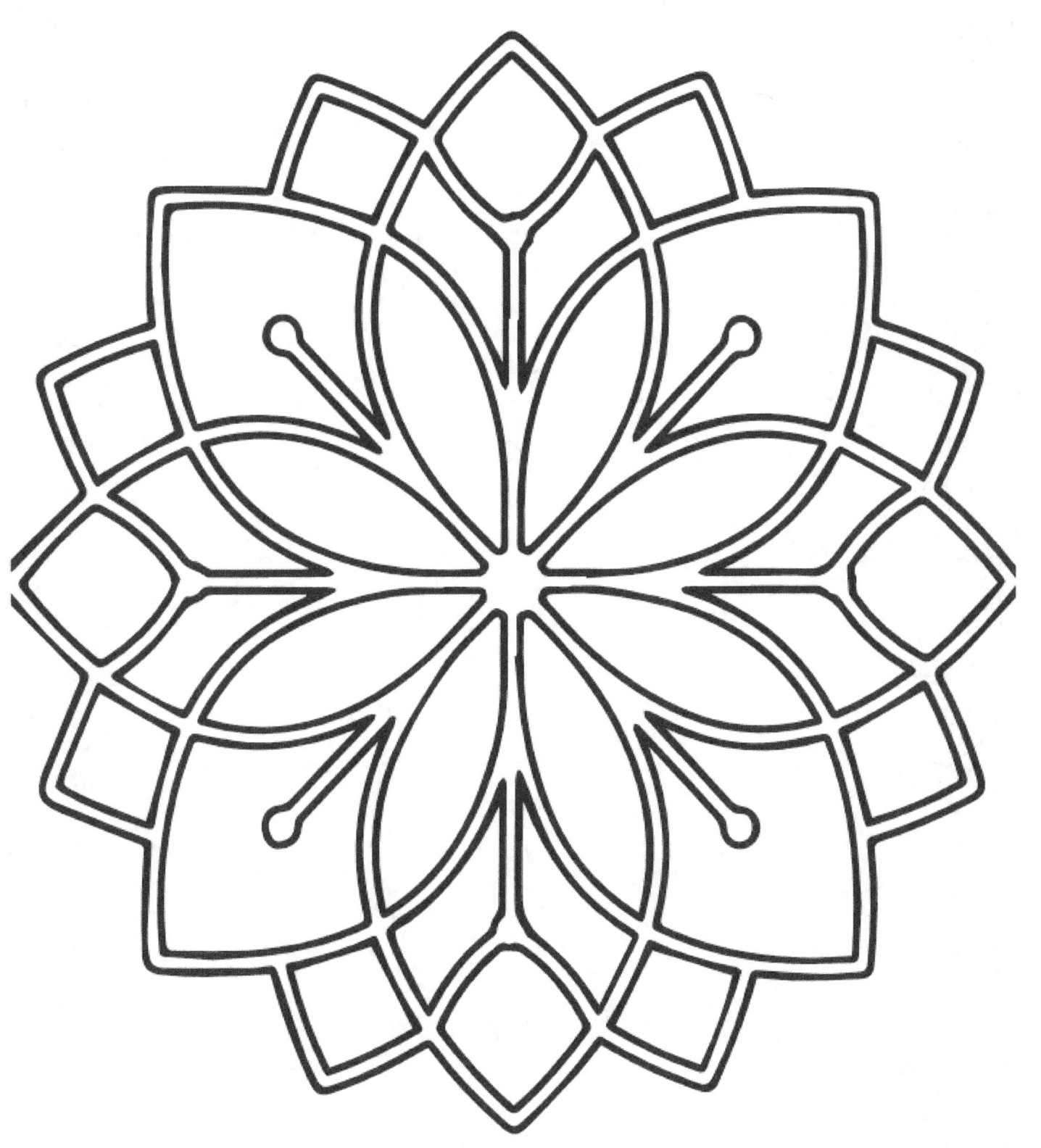

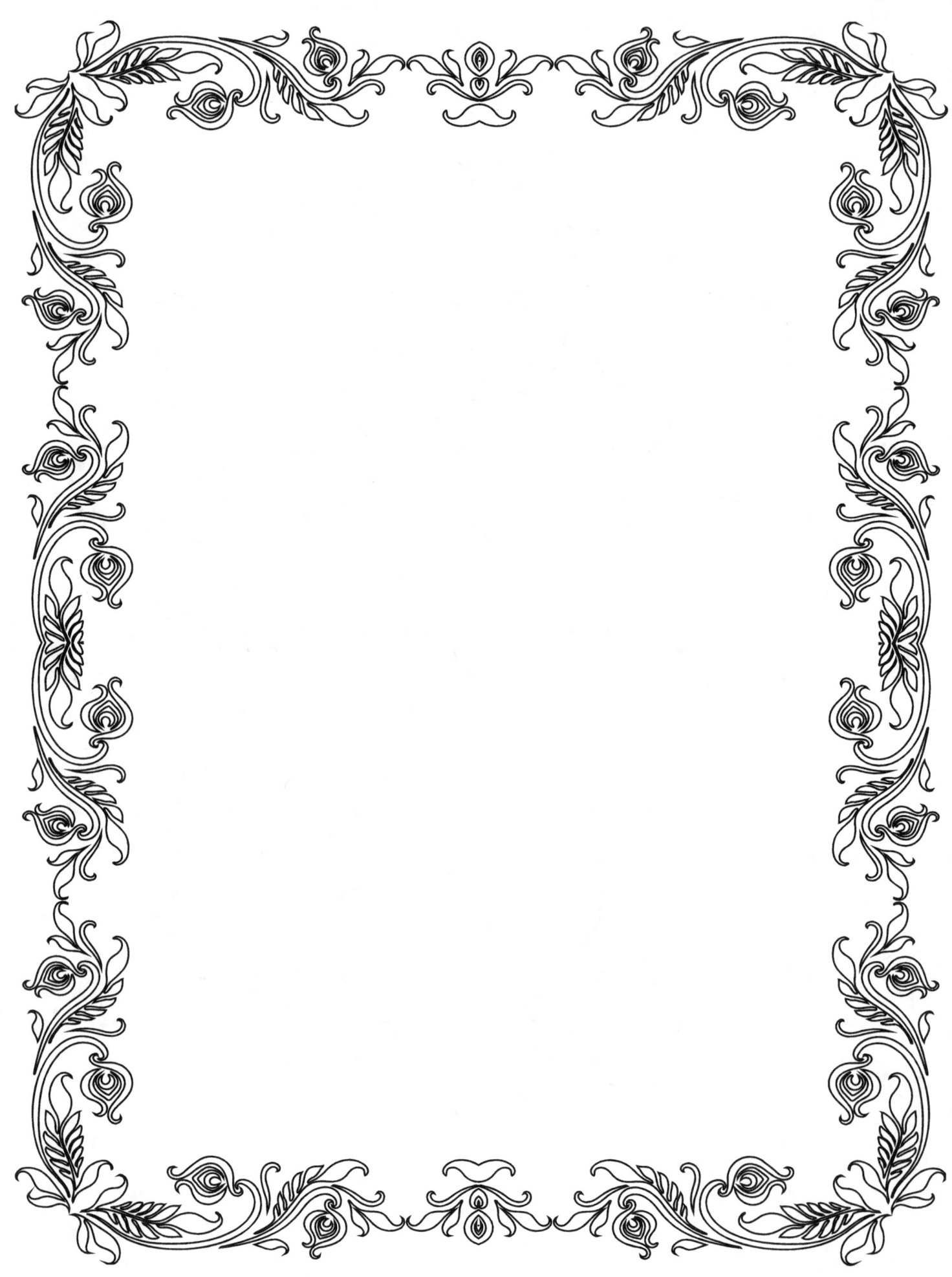

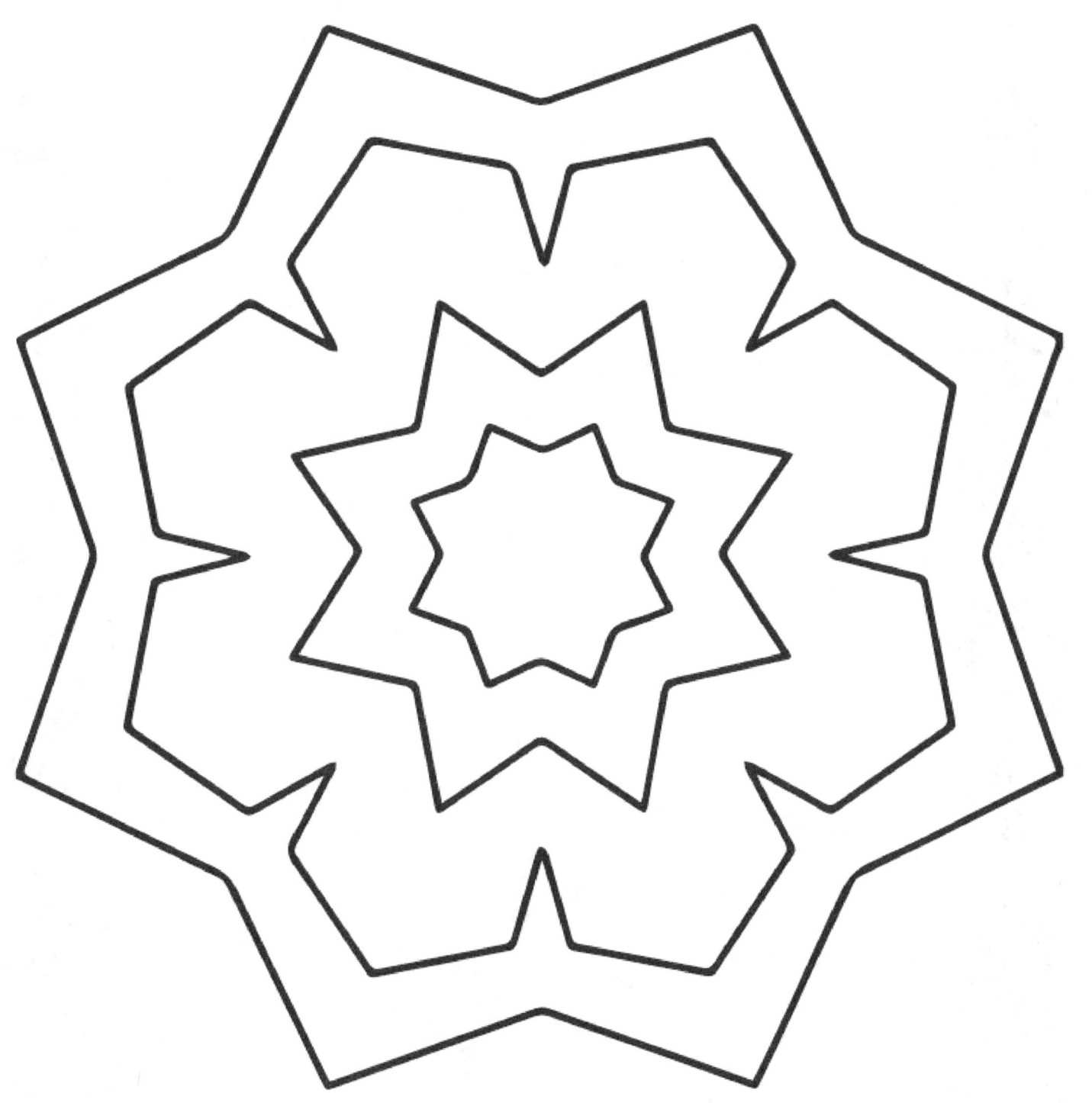

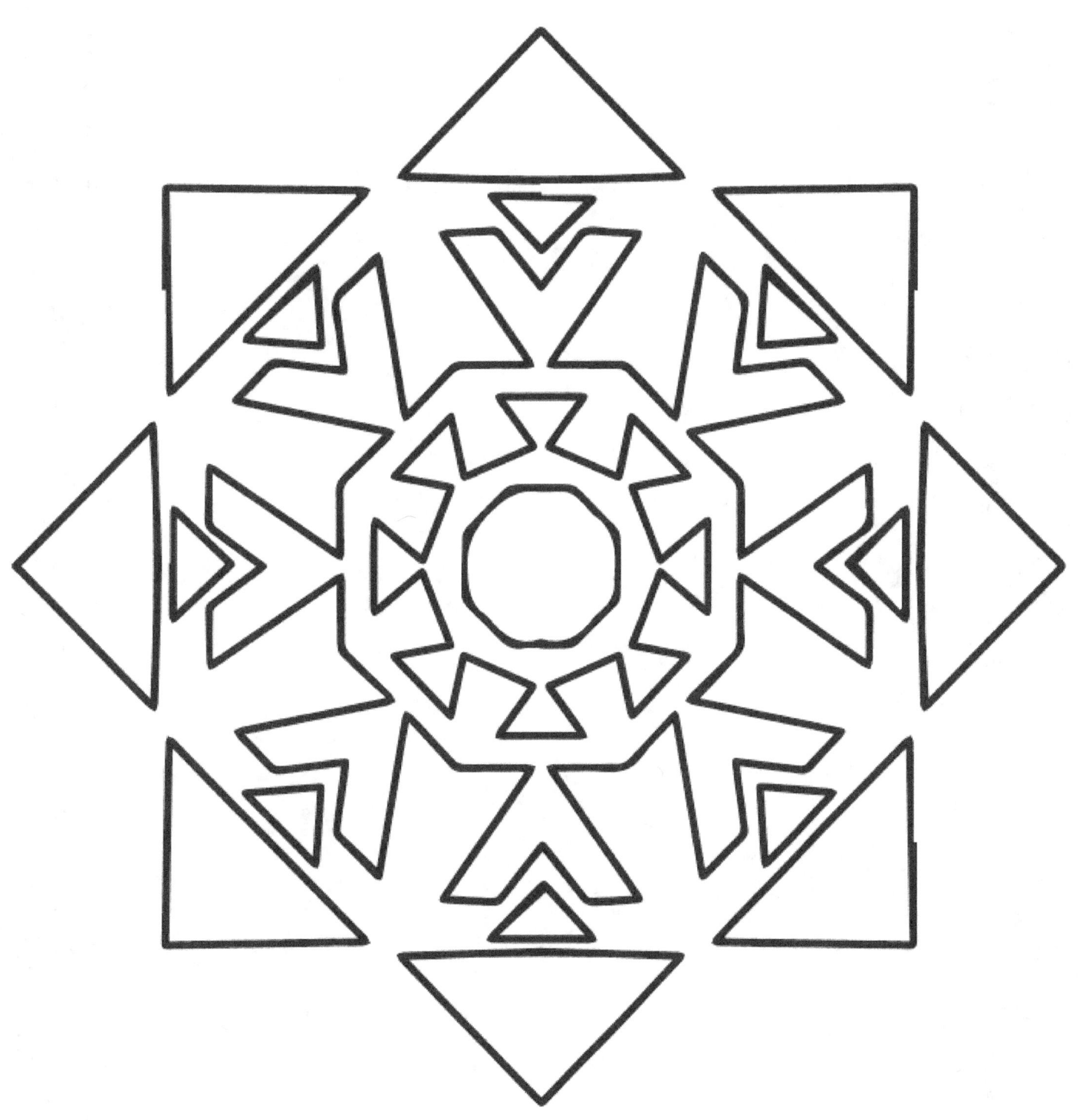

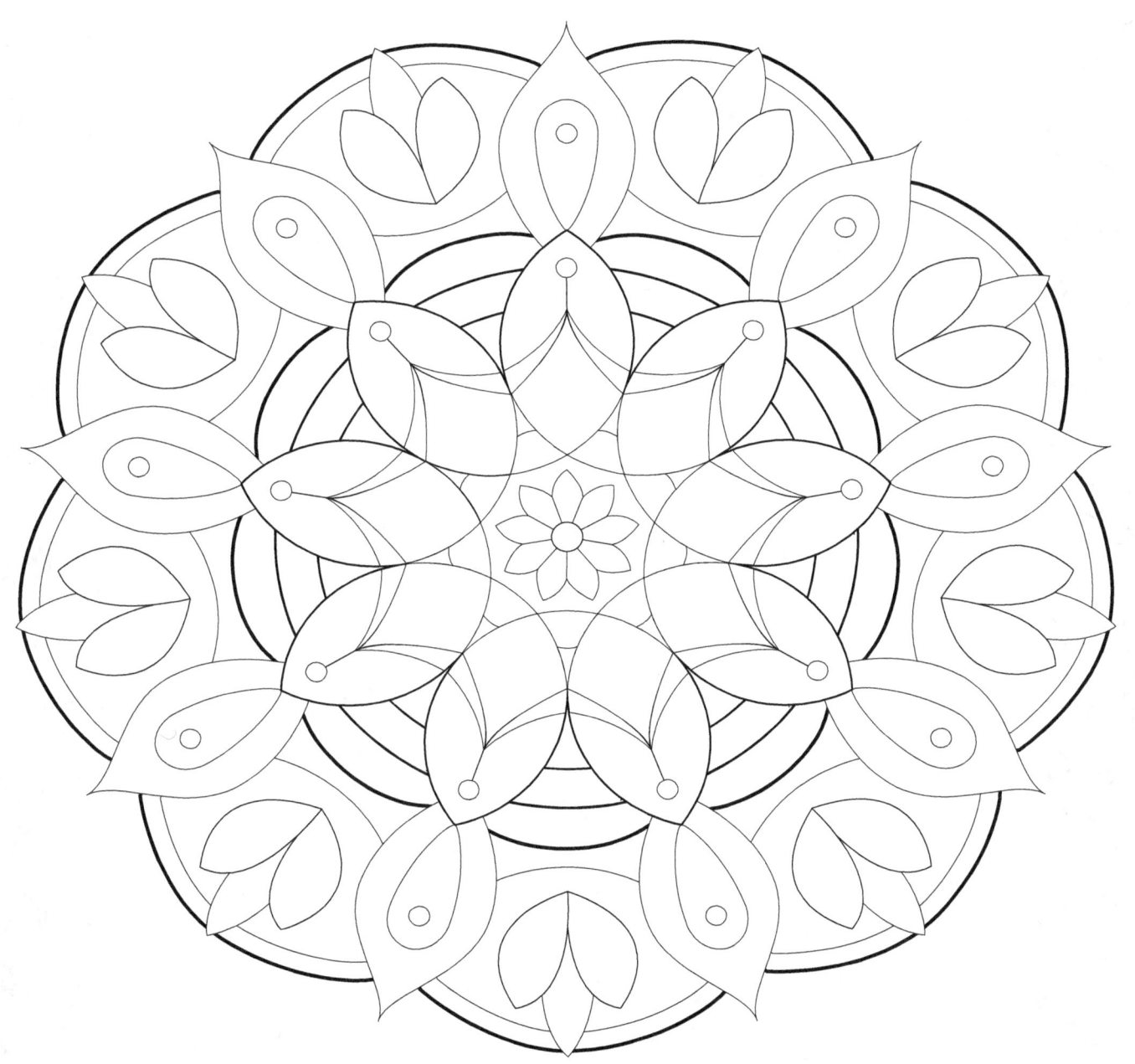

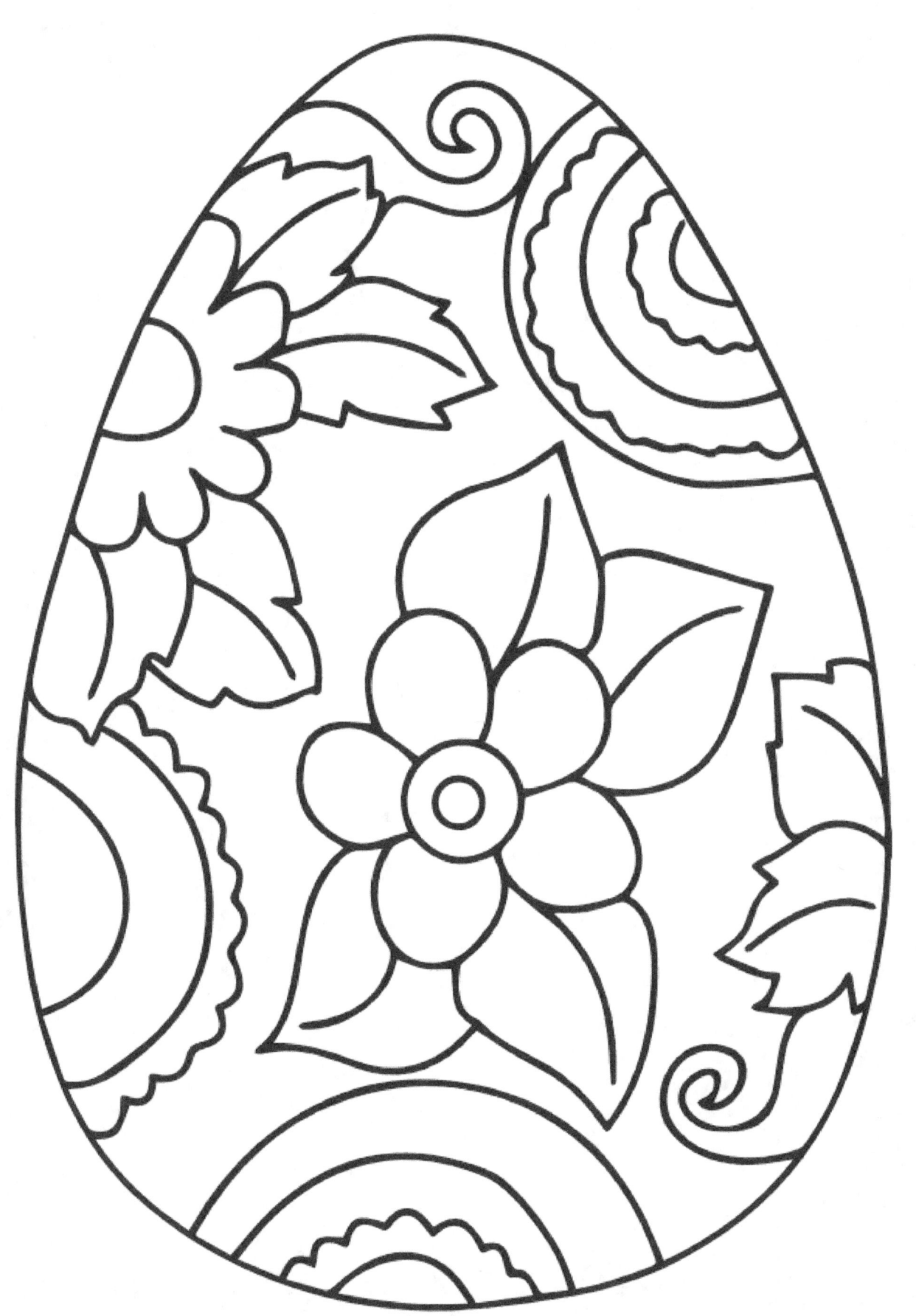

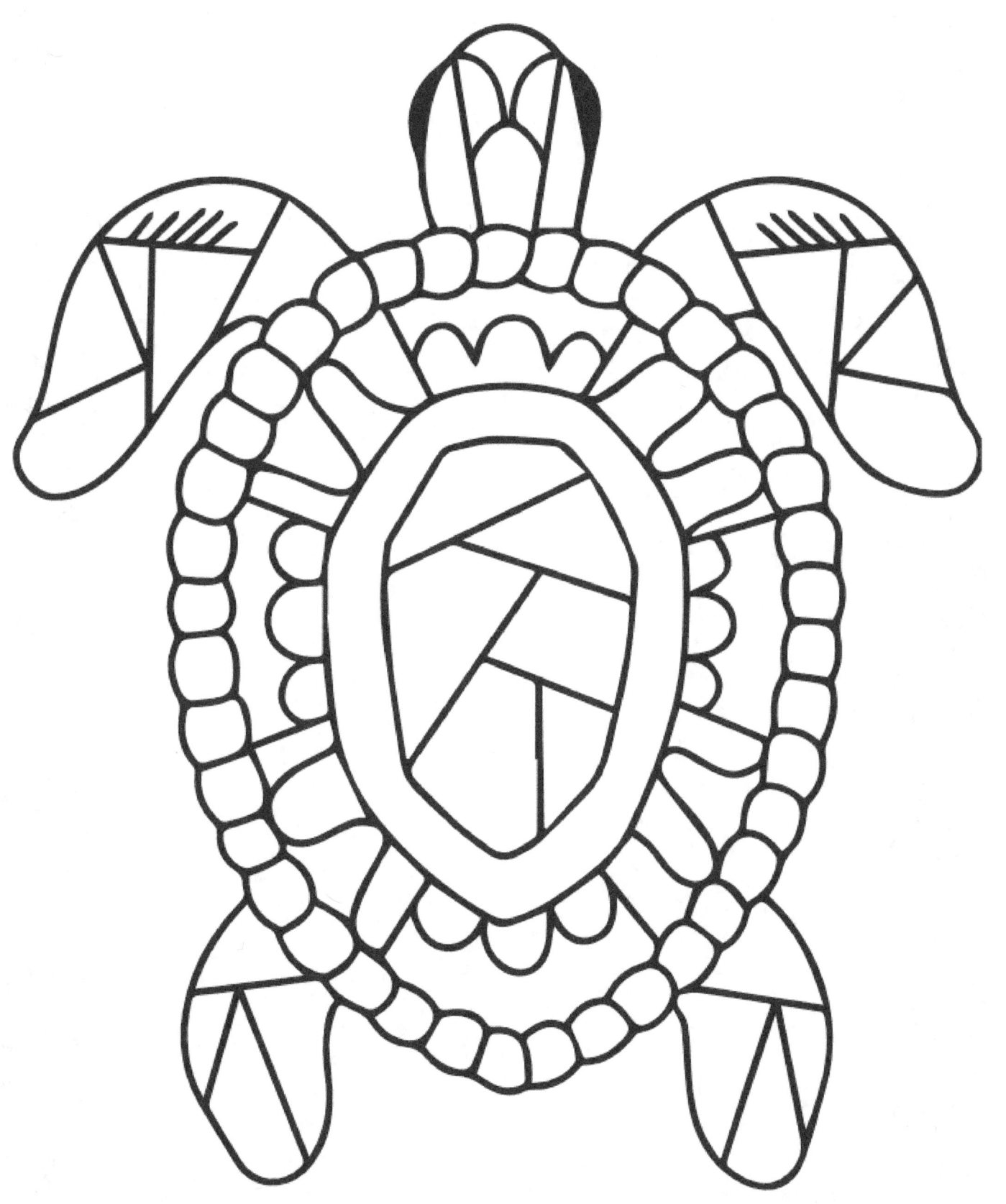

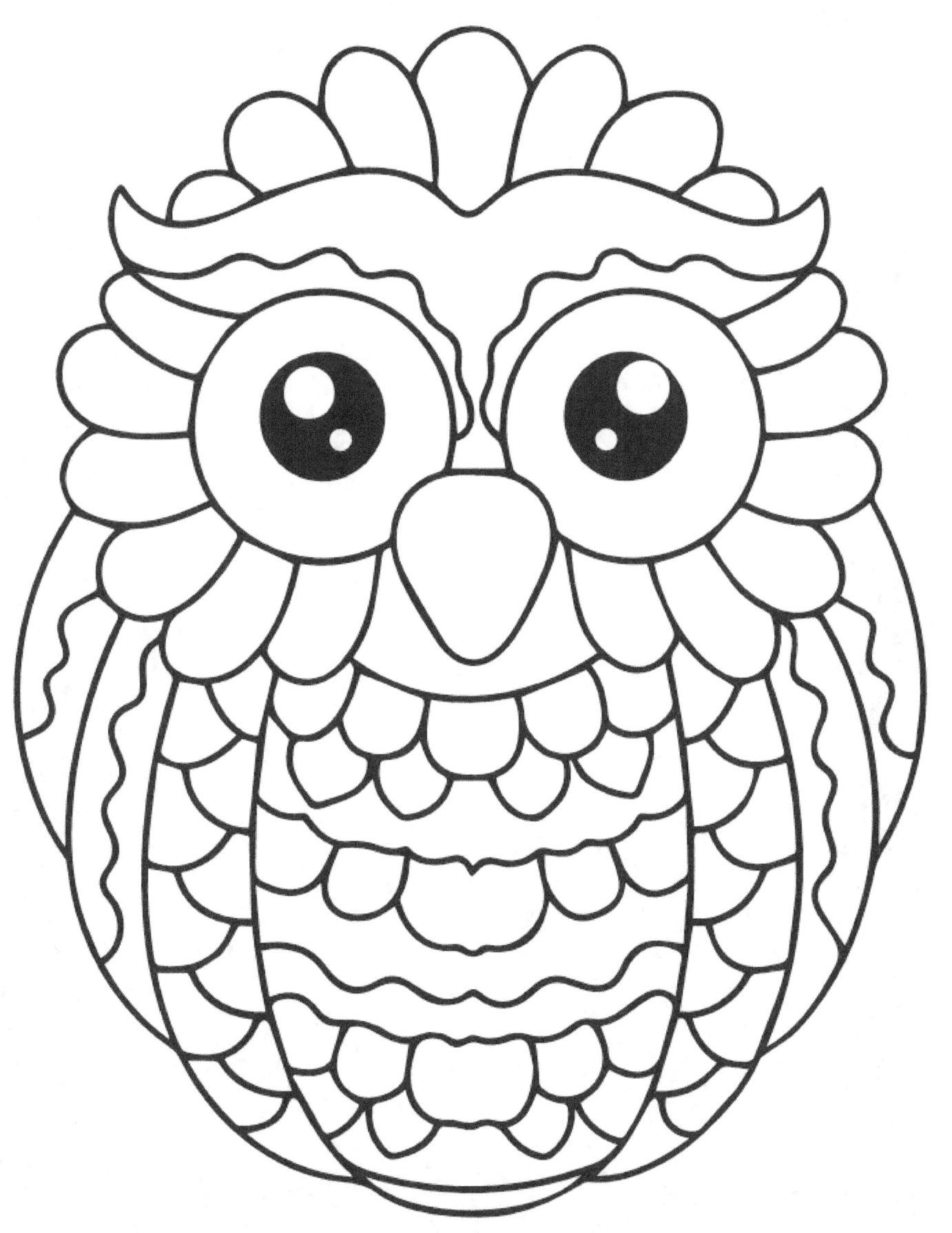

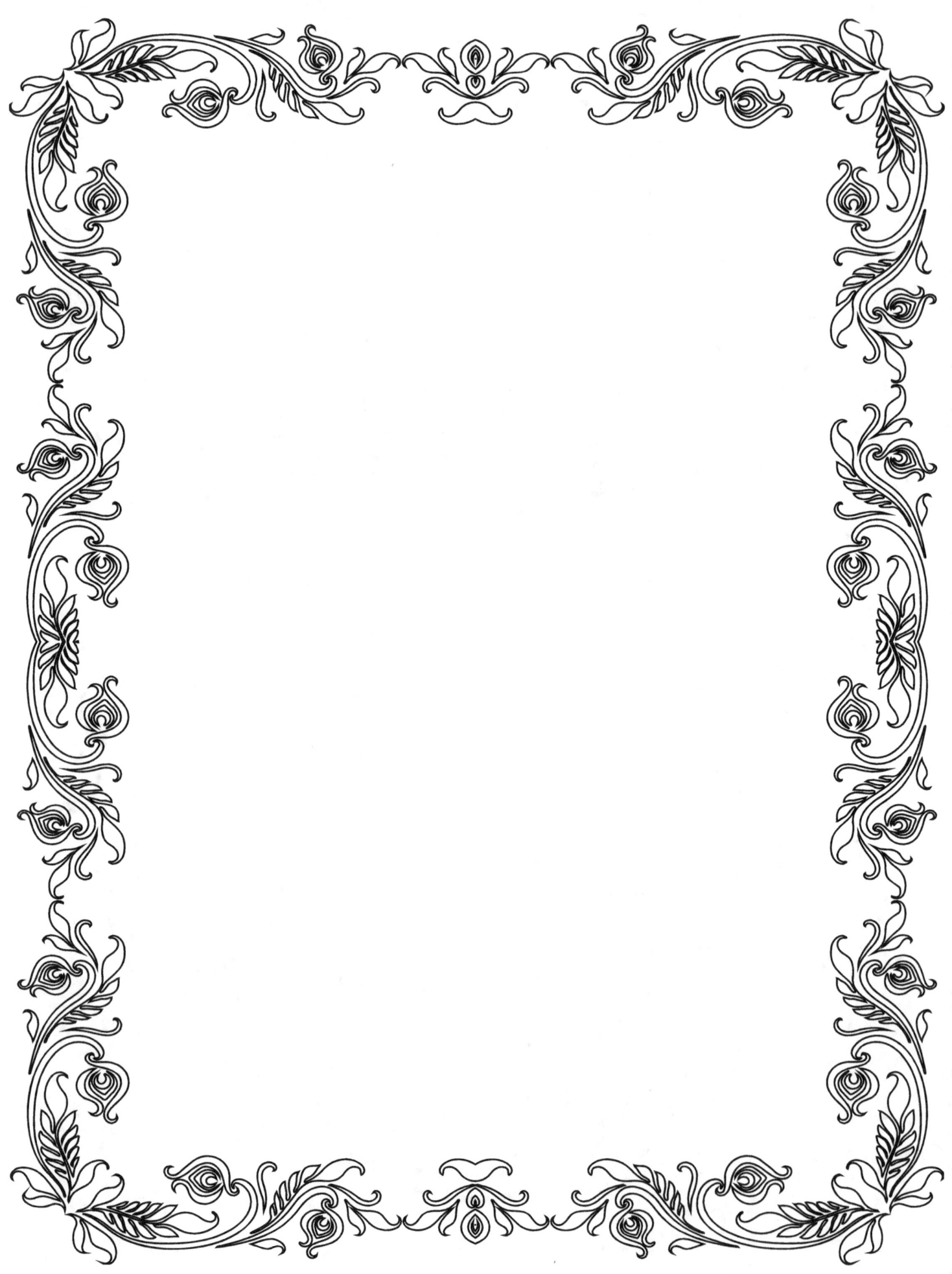

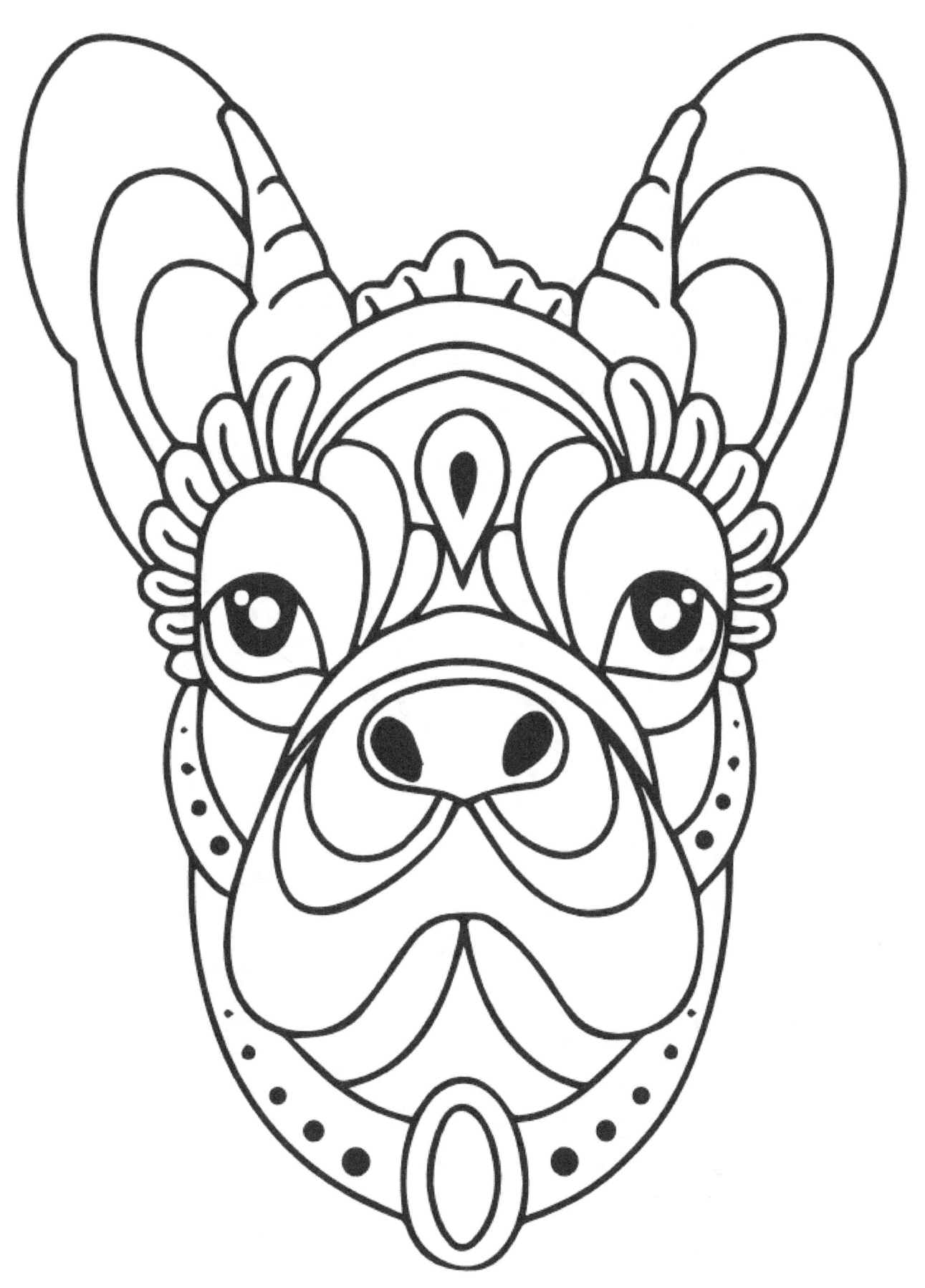